Cliques, Phonies, & Other Baloney

by Trevor Romain

D0104591

free spirit
PUBLISHING®

Library of Congress Cataloging-in-Publication Data
Romain, Trevor.
    Cliques, phonies, and other baloney / Trevor Romain.
        p.   cm.
    Summary: Discusses cliques, what they are and their negative aspects, and gives advice on forming healthier relationships and friendships.
    ISBN-13 978-1-57542-045-5
    ISBN-10 1-57542-045-7
    1. Interpersonal relations in children—Juvenile literature. 2. Cliques (Sociology)—Juvenile literature. 3. Friendship in children—Juvenile literature. [1. Cliques (Sociology) 2. Social groups. 3. Interpersonal relations. 4. Friendship.] I. Title.
BF723.I646R65 1998
758.2'5—dc21   98-36248
                                                                                               CIP
                                                                                               AC

ISBN: 978-1-57542-045-5

Reading Level Grade 3; Interest Level Ages 8–13;
Fountas & Pinnell Guided Reading Level O

25 24 23 22 21 20
Printed in the United States of America
S18860615

Free Spirit Publishing Inc.
217 Fifth Avenue North, Suite 200
Minneapolis, MN 55401-1299
(612) 338-2068
help4kids@freespirit.com
www.freespirit.com

Dedication

For my young friend, Candy,
a true survivor and a fighter
who never gives up.

Contents

Introduction

Since this is the introduction, I'd like to introduce something. It's a word that's spelled funny and sounds funny, and can actually be a pain in the neck. The word is "clique." It sounds like "trick." It's tricky being "cliquey" as you go through school.

Why? Because cliques can make you feel:

- lonely
- scared
- angry
- unwelcome
- unhappy
- unpopular

When you feel this way, it's hard to have fun, pay attention in school, or feel good about yourself.

If you're bothered by cliques, this book is for you. If you're dying to be in a clique, this book is for you, too. Even if you're in a clique, you can learn something from this book.

This book is about cliques—what they are, what they do, and what *you* can do about *them*. It's also about making friends (those important people in your life who don't mind if you act like a big dork, say the wrong thing, or make a mistake). You'll learn that having good friends isn't always the same thing as being popular or being in a clique. You'll also discover that the best way to get along with people—at school or anywhere else—is to be self-confident and friendly.

Just What Is a Clique?

CLIQUE (noun): a small, closely knit group of people who share things in common.

That definition sounds harmless. So why do some cliques leave you feeling annoyed, uneasy, and even a little queasy?

If cliques make you sick, you might have *Cliques Vomititus,* otherwise known as the Clique Sickness. Or maybe you feel like throwing up because the clique is being cliquey. This means the clique members might:

1. Leave other kids out on purpose, and
2. Act like they're better than everyone else—including you.

Cliquey (the Dreaded C-Word)

Not all cliques are cliquey, but many are. Experts say that some cliques behave like this to feel stronger and more powerful. Kids in the clique might feel better about themselves if they say, "Let's not hang out with *that* person."

Being cliquey can make the clique feel secure (because being part of a group is a kind of protection). Think about how wild dogs form packs in the wilderness, or how gangs hang out in the streets. Cliques aren't as dangerous, but the idea is the same. They stick together because there's safety in numbers.

The #1 Clique Myth

Kids in cliques are the most confident,
happy, and popular kids of all.

The Truth: Some clique members may be confident and feel good about themselves. But others may be insecure, which is why being part of a group might make them feel better.

It's also a myth that kids in cliques are always popular. Actually, they may have trouble getting to know other kids in their class or school if they hang out with the same people all the time.

Four Dorky Things Cliques Do

#1: They always travel in a group. They go everywhere together, like a herd of cows.

Why do they want to behave like a big animal
that says "Moo"?

#2: They have rules. The rules say who's cool and who's not, and what members can and can't do.

Some of the rules are really stupid. I heard about a clique where members pulled out their eyelashes so they would look scary. Duh! Imagine trying to blink in a sandstorm without eyelashes. Besides, who needs **MORE** rules at school?

#3: They have leaders. The leaders make rules that everyone has to follow.

Aren't cliques too old for Follow the Leader?

#4: They have a dress code. Most people in the clique wear the same kinds of shoes, T-shirts, jeans, jackets, and caps.

They might have to wear pants so baggy that
three people, a dog, and a gigantic Nerf ball
could fit into a single pair.

Try this out: Say the word "clique" to yourself ten times fast. You sound like a machine or a robot. Hmmmm—what does that tell you?

Some cliques act like they **RULE** the **SCHOOL**. (Or the neighborhood. Or the mall. Or the basketball court. Or whatever.) Maybe they pick on certain people or treat them like dirt. In fact, maybe they even treat *you* that way.

Why does this happen? Is it because cliques are full of mean, nasty, horrible people? (Not really.) Is it because their main goal in life is to make you miserable? (Nope.)

Understanding Cliques

To understand cliques, you have to know why they exist. Figuring out the why can make things easier to understand. It's kind of like taking a car engine apart to see how it works, or studying a skeleton to learn about the human body.

Cliques exist because everyone, no matter what age, wants to have friends. People like to feel they belong.

Strange But True

People will do the strangest things to belong or fit in. Take me, for example. When I was in eighth grade, I wanted to join the Smoking Clique in the worst way. I thought those people were cool and tough, and I wanted to hang out with them. So I tried smoking once and nearly barfed. It was gross! I learned that smoking cigarettes wasn't a good way to make friends.

Next, I decided to jump around and act silly to get my classmates to notice me. This turned into a disaster when my pants fell down in front of a whole group of people! I realized that being a fool isn't cool, either.

Another way I tried to make friends and fit in was by pretending my family was really rich.
I told a group of kids at school that I lived in a mansion with an Olympic-sized, heated pool because I wanted them to think I was important. Everyone was impressed, until the group paid me a surprise visit. I lived in a small house, and the closest thing to a swimming pool in my yard was a birdbath. I felt bad when the other kids found out. I was pretending to be what I thought they wanted me to be, but I was really just being a phony.

Phonies and Fakes

What's a phony? Someone who's being a fake. Someone who isn't the "real thing." If you see someone acting, talking, dressing, or behaving a certain way just to go along with the crowd (or clique), the person is probably being phony.

I once knew a girl who pretended she played guitar in a band, even though she knew nothing about the guitar. She tried hard to be cool—she wore long earrings, black clothes, and dark glasses (even indoors). One day, the group she hung out with asked her to play guitar for them, and she had to make up an excuse. She acted like her finger was sprained, and she walked around with a bandaged finger for three weeks to fool everyone. The day she took off the bandage, her friends asked her to join their band. What could she do but tell the truth? She was embarrassed and felt like a big phony.

How to Spot a Phony

Phonies . . .

Pretend to be someone they're not.

Have an image to uphold.

Only care about impressing others.

Need lots of approval.

YUCK!

Phonies are easy to recognize. They stick out like blue M&M's on a double cheese pizza.

Are You a Phony?
A Quiz

1. Do you put on an act to make people think you're cool? yes no

2. Do you tell people what you think they want to hear even if you don't mean it? yes no

3. Will you do almost anything just to be liked? yes no

4. Do you make up lies to impress people? yes no

5. Are you being honest on this quiz? yes no

Did you answer yes to the questions on the quiz? Then you're not being the **TRUE YOU.** If you worry about showing the world who you really are, you're not alone. Lots of kids feel the same way.

If you're being a phony or fake, it may be because you think it's a way to fit in or be accepted by a clique. But why pretend to be someone else? Being a fake is like wearing a mask all the time. It can get uncomfortable in there.

I can't breathe in this thing!

Being Yourself

To be yourself, you have to *know* yourself.* What do you believe in? What are your likes and dislikes? What are your favorite activities, and why? What are you good at? How do you have fun? What lifts your spirits? What makes you feel positive and happy?

*It also helps to *like* yourself.

If you like who you are, you'll feel more self-confident. When you're confident, it shows. You can look people in the eye, hold your head high, and speak your mind. You feel good inside and out. Best of all, people will like you for *you*.

Real Friends

lemonade 50¢

Kids who have friends feel better about themselves and are happier than kids who don't. That's because friends offer help and support. Friends are good to talk to, and they're fun to be around.

When somebody else likes you, it's easier for **YOU** to like you, and the world becomes a nicer place to be in (if you know what I mean). If you don't know what on earth I'm talking about, read this page again, but slowly this time.

What Are "Real" Friends?

Real friends like the *real* you. You don't have to impress them or be phony around them. That's the great thing about friends.

Real friends accept you as you are. They're there
for you when you're upset or have a problem.
They keep your secrets and know what makes you
laugh. Best of all, they *care* about you, and you
care about them.

Friends vs. Cliques*

Is there a difference between a group of friends and a clique? There can be. But first, take a look at some of the things cliques and groups of friends have in common. Being part of a clique or a friendship group can:

- help you learn to get along with others
- give you a chance to do projects together, be social, and have fun
- let you become close to other kids, learn about each other, and trust each other.

*The small print: Cliques aren't *all* bad. They really do have some positive benefits (like the ones mentioned above).

BUT (and it's a really *BIG* but) . . .

The difference is that cliques tend to make members *conform*. This means you might have to think, act, talk, and dress like everyone else in the clique. The result? You might feel like a phony—like you have to be the way other people *expect* . . . instead of being yourself.

P.S. Some cliques also make other kids feel unwelcome. They *exclude* people, or leave them out.

Are You Hanging Out with the Wrong People?

Ask yourself these questions:

- Do I feel like I have to behave a certain way to be accepted?
- Do I feel like a fake?
- Does the group discourage me from making other friends?
- Does it seem like I always have to meet the approval of others in the group?
- Do I feel out of place with these people?

If you answered yes to any of these questions, you might want to think about finding other friends. You can form a new friendship circle with kids who let you just be you—also known as *real* friends.

It's time for me to make new friends.

Friendship Pointers

If you want new friends (or more friends), all you've got to do is look. Your friends don't all have to go to the same school as you. They don't have to be the same age, gender, or race as you. Your friend can be a kid who's in a grade above or below yours, or even an elderly neighbor. Your friend can be a boy or girl. You'd be amazed by how much you can learn from people who aren't just like you.

Friendships don't just happen. It takes effort on your part to make friends and keep them. In fact, being a friend is something you can work on a little bit each day.

Do's and Don'ts for Making Friends

DO talk to people. If you're shy at first, just say something friendly like, "Your new backpack is cool." Or ask a question like, "Do you know what tonight's homework is?" With practice, starting a conversation will become easier.

DON'T stay inside by yourself all day watching TV, picking your nose, playing video games, or sitting in front of the computer. You won't meet any new people, and a spider might build a web on your head.

DO try to make other people feel good. Ask questions to show you're interested in them. You can try something like, "I noticed you're really good at art. Do you have some drawings you could show me sometime?"

DON'T walk up to someone and say something like, "Be my friend or you'll be sorry!" You can't force someone to be friends with you.

DO invite people to join you. Ask some kids to come to your house to watch videos, invite someone to sit with you at lunch, or start a club and find out if other people want to join. This will help people get to know you better.

DON'T invite your whole class over for an all-you-can-eat pizza party, order 35 pepperoni pizzas on your mom's credit card, and feed the leftovers to the dog. This will only aggravate your parents.

DO be a good listener. If you're the one doing all the talking, chances are you're boring somebody (maybe even yourself). To be a good listener, you have to really *listen* to other people and *hear* what they say. Look the person in the eye and nod your head to show you understand.

DON'T brag about yourself, hog the spotlight, and show off—and then, when everyone ignores you, simply turn up the volume and talk even **LOUDER**. You'll only drive people away.

DO talk to the "new kid." If you've ever moved to a new neighborhood or gone to a different school, you know how it feels to be new (lonely, strange, and scary). Make an effort to get to know the new kids, and they'll like you right away. Show them around school or the neighborhood, sit with them at lunch, and introduce them to other people you know.

DON'T overdo it. (There's such a thing as being *too* friendly.) If you get right in the new person's face and say: "Hi! I'd really like to be your friend because you're new here, and I think you look like a really nice person, and I need a friend right now, and blah, blah, blah, and on and on . . . " you're saying too much too fast. If spit flies out of your mouth, take a deep breath and slow down.

DO include people. Remember, cliques tend to leave people out—that means they're usually picky about who can hang around them. It's much more friendly to *include* people—even if you don't know them well, and even if they're different from you.

DON'T walk around calling people dorks, losers, dopes, nerds, dunderheads, dweebs, wimps, or other mean names. It's not a friendly thing to do, and you might get a reputation as someone to avoid.

Here's a really **BIG** tip for making friends:

BE FRIENDLY!

Five Ways to Be Friendly

#1: Smile! It's better than walking around with a scowl on your face.

#2: Say hi to people in the hall and in class—even if you don't know them very well.

At first, you might get some funny looks (like "Do I *know* this person?"), but soon everyone will realize you're just trying to be friendly.

#3: Compliment at least one person each day. Just don't say something like, "Wow, your hair looks really good—for a change."

#4: Be a good sport about losing a game or any other competition. It's much more friendly than stomping off the field and shouting at the top of your lungs, "I can't believe we lost to a bunch of wimps like them!"

#5: Talk to people before or after class, or when you're at your locker, waiting for the bus, or in line. Each person you talk to is a potential friend.

TIP: Avoid talking to people *during* class. Teachers hate that.

What does all this add up to? Good people skills. Having good people skills means being cheerful, kind, outgoing, generous, or funny.

Polishing Your People Skills

You can develop people skills, if you don't already have them. How? Become a People Magnet. Smile at people you meet, laugh a lot, show your confidence, be kind to your class-mates, listen to your teachers, and don't be afraid to be you. You'll attract people like a magnet. Maybe you'll even become . . .

POPULAR.

What's Popularity?

Good question!

Many kids, more than anything else, want to be popular. Have you ever thought:

- "I wish I was popular."
- "If I was popular, I'd be happy."
- "So-and-so is much more popular than I am."
- "My life would be so much better if I was popular!"

Popular. Popular. Popular. Popular. It sounds funny if you say it over and over in your head. Like "clique," "popular" is a strange word.

The Truth About Popularity

Being popular *can* be fun. You might feel important and well-liked. Popularity can make you feel
like you belong and have lots of things to do.

But many kids think popularity is *way* more important than it is. Here are just a few things that are even more important:

- your family
- your schoolwork
- your hobbies
- your pet
- your goals and dreams
- and, most of all, your opinion of yourself.

Want to hear some top-secret, surprising, shocking news?!

Tell me!

When people wish to be popular, often what they *really* want is to feel good about themselves.

Maybe you think the popular kids are the coolest people in the world. Maybe you believe you're a big nobody. Not true! You're a unique and special person with a lot to offer the world. You just need to tell yourself that . . . and believe it.

Popularity Pop Quiz

True or false? The popular kids are always:

1. the best looking.

2. the best dressed.

3. the most athletic.

4. the happiest.

5. the strongest.

6. the richest.

7. the coolest.

8. the most talented.

9. the smartest.

10. able to leap tall buildings in a single bound.

Answers: 1. false 2. false 3. false 4. false 5. false 6. false 7. false 8. false 9. false 10. false.

Many of the popular kids you know may be good-looking, good at sports, well-dressed, and more, but these qualities don't *guarantee* popularity. Face it, someone could be super gorgeous and the world's best athlete and still have a terrible personality. This kind of person might not be very popular. It's not only what's on the outside that counts; what's *inside* matters more.

Think Positive (About Yourself)

Do you spend time worrying about whether you're popular? Do you often tell yourself that other kids are better than you? Stop! Halt!

CUT IT OUT!

Instead, focus on feeling good about yourself. You can turn your negative thoughts into positive ones. Try this:

Instead of:
"Nobody likes me."

Tell yourself:
"I have friends who really care about me. That's more important than trying to make *everybody* like me."

Two Popularity Myths

Myth #1: Popular people are better than everyone else.

TOTALLY UNTRUE! HOGWASH! NONSENSE! RUBBISH!

Popular people aren't better than everyone else. Kids who are popular are still human—they have problems, hopes, dreams, worries, fears, good days, and bad days just like other people do.

I hope my teacher likes my report.

Myth #2: To be popular, you need to treat some kids badly.

BALONEY!

Popularity isn't about making other people feel *unpopular*. And it's not about telling other kids they're not good enough to hang around you. You can be popular *and* a nice person at the same time.

A Question for You

Are you popular with yourself? (Don't worry, this isn't a trick question.) If you base your self-esteem on what *other* people think of you, instead of what *you* think of you, you'll always feel like you don't measure up. Or you'll spend a lot of time trying to please everyone. Either way, you're being too hard on yourself.

A Few Words of Advice

Be yourself. Learn to like yourself.
Be kind to other people.
That's the *real* secret to popularity.

Tips, Tricks, and Helpful Hints

What do cliques and popularity have in common? Many kids want to be popular or in a clique because *the need to belong* is so strong. They want to be accepted, approved of, and admired. (Maybe this is how you feel most of the time.) It's perfectly normal to want to belong. In fact, it's human nature.

But what happens when the **IN** crowd leaves you **OUT?** Or what if no matter how friendly you are, a clique decides to snub you or tries to make you feel bad about yourself?

Uh-oh, you're dealing with a **BAD CLIQUE.**

Bad Cliques Are No Good

A bad clique can *really* make you sick. You might feel queasy (like you just ate too much candy) or scared (like you have a big math test that—**YIKES!**—you forgot to study for).

You might even feel like doing something mean and nasty—something that might make the clique feel as rotten as you do.

HELPFUL HINT: This is a *verrrry* bad idea.

The Four Worst Tricks
for Dealing with Bad Cliques

#1: Ignoring the clique. That's like cleaning your room by cramming your stuff in your closet and slamming the door shut. Sooner or later, you have to open the door—**WHOA! LOOK OUT!** You'll feel better if you face your problems, instead of pretending they don't exist.

#2: Getting back at the clique. Don't launch a spoonful of peas at the "popular" lunch table. This will only make people mad at you.

#3: Making enemies of the clique. If you try to threaten or embarrass the clique members, you might end up as a moving target, running for cover in the school hallways. (Then you'll feel even *more* sick when you have to go to school.)

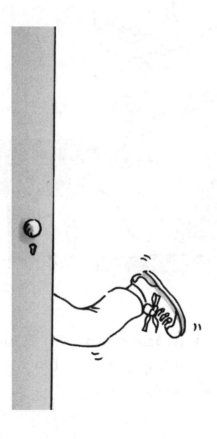

#4: Being a phony to impress the clique.

People can smell a phony a mile away. It's better to just be yourself.

Extra! Extra!
Important Announcement!

Don't let a bad clique spoil a perfectly good day.

If you're on the outs with a clique or with the popular crowd, you may feel sad and rejected. But
you *do* have a choice for handling the situation.
(No, you don't have to pack your bags and move
to Antarctica!)

You can. . .

DARE TO BE DIFFERENT.

Being Different Is Okay

Being different doesn't mean you're weird, dorky, or unpopular. It means you're an independent thinker—an individual. It means you believe you're a very interesting, creative, thoughtful, worthwhile person . . . with or without a crowd.

How do you learn to be an individual? Start by believing in yourself. Find your strengths and make the most of them. When I was growing up, I was shy and had trouble making friends. I learned that I could tell jokes and make people laugh, so I worked on my sense of humor. This helped me gain confidence and gave me a way to reach out to others.

(**TIP:** If you want to make people laugh, you can tell jokes or funny stories. Just make sure you're laughing *with* people, not *at* them. And don't be afraid to laugh at yourself.)

You can also get involved with other kids who seem fun and interesting—maybe even *outside* of your school. Join a team, be a Girl Scout or Boy Scout, find a community club, or become a volunteer. When you're involved in lots of activities, you have a better chance of meeting other people and learning new things about yourself.

116

Friendship Matters

Remember, you always have choices about your friendships. You can find other kids to hang out with if a clique doesn't want you—or if you don't want the clique. You can decide that being popular with your *friends* is the only popularity that really matters. It's up to you.

If you have one or two good friends, that's great! But you don't have to stop there. Use your people skills to make a few more friends. After all, you can never have too many people who care about you and like you for who you are.

The Top Ten Ways to Keep Your Friends

10. Show them kindness and respect.

9. Stick up for them.

8. Be supportive when your friends need help or advice.

7. Tell the truth (but be kind about it).

6. If you hurt a friend, say you're sorry.

5. If a friend hurts you and apologizes, accept the apology.

4. If you make a promise, keep it.

3. Put some effort into your friendships; otherwise your friends might feel neglected.

2. Don't try to change your friends—accept them the way they are.

1. Treat your friends the way you want them to treat you.

And one more thing:
Always be thankful for your friends.

Resources

BOOKS

Bullies Are a Pain in the Brain by Trevor Romain (Minneapolis: Free Spirit Publishing, 1997). Is a clique *bullying* you (teasing, pushing, hurting, or picking on you)? Then you need to know how to protect yourself. This book offers tips and practical suggestions, and explains how to become "Bully-Proof."

Coping with Cliques by Lee A. Peck (NY: The Rosen Publishing Group, 1992). This helpful book covers the pros and cons of cliques, and offers basic advice for making friends.

How Kids Make Friends . . . Secrets for Making Lots of Friends, No Matter How Shy You Are by Lonnie Michelle (Buffalo Grove, IL: Freedom Publishing Company, 1995). The author shares secrets for making friends, overcoming shyness, and becoming more confident.

Popularity Has Its Ups and Downs by Meg F. Schneider (NY: Julian Messner, 1991). You'll learn about the myths and dangers of popularity and find out how to develop a better sense of self-worth.

Stick Up for Yourself! Every Kid's Guide to Personal Power and Positive Self-Esteem by Gershen Kaufman, Ph.D., Lev Raphael, Ph.D., and Pamela Espeland (Minneapolis: Free Spirit Publishing, 1999). Learn how to stick up for yourself in all sorts of situations, build stronger relationships, and feel good about who you are.

The Ultimate Kids' Club Book: How to Organize, Find Members, Run Meetings, Raise Money, Handle Problems, and Much More! by Melissa Maupin (Minneapolis: Free Spirit Publishing, 1996). Starting a club is a great way to meet new people and make friends. This book will tell you everything you need to know to start a club and make it last.

ORGANIZATIONS

Big Brothers/Big Sisters of America
National Office
PO Box 141599
Irving, TX 75014
(469) 351-3100
www.bbbs.org

If you're looking for an older friend who can provide
guidance and support, you can get a Big Sister or Big
Brother. These adult mentors not only spend time with
you but also can serve as important role models.

Boy Scouts of America
1325 West Walnut Hill Lane
Irving, TX 75015-2079
(972) 580-2000
www.scouting.org

Scouting is a great way to get to know other boys and
form strong friendships. This program for boys and
young men helps to build character and fitness
through fun, educational activities.

Girl Scouts of the U.S.A.
420 Fifth Avenue
New York, NY 10018-2798
1-800-478-7248
www.girlscouts.org

Girls who get involved in this program learn to become individuals and build stronger relationships with others. All sorts of activities (from camping to leadership) are offered.

Peace Pals
26 Benton Road
Wassaic, NY 12592
(845) 877-6093
www.wppspeacepals.org

You can find friends in faraway places. If you'd like to find a friend who lives in another part of the world, you could get a pen pal through this organization.

About the Author/Illustrator

When South African-born Trevor Romain was 12, his teacher told him he wasn't talented enough to do art. By accident, he found out 20 years later that he could draw. Since that lucky day, he has written and illustrated more than 30 books for children. In addition to writing, illustrating, drinking tea, and trying to avoid trouble, Trevor regularly visits schools to speak to children, and he spends his free time with kids who have cancer at the Brackenridge Hospital in Austin, Texas. He receives hundreds of letters annually from principals, teachers, and students who have been touched by his humor and energy.

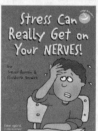

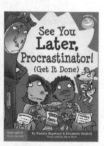

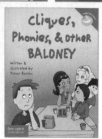